PRINCE EDWARD ISLAND

JOURNEY ACROSS CANADA

Harry Beckett

The Rourke Book Co., Inc.
Vero Beach, Florida 32964

Harry Beckett M.A. (Cambridge), M.Ed. (Toronto), Dip.Ed. (Hull, England) has taught at the elementary and high school levels in England, Canada, France, and Germany. He has also travelled widely for a tour operator and a major book company.

Edited by Laura Edlund
Laura Edlund received her B.A. in English literature from the University of Toronto and studied Writing for Multimedia and Book Editing and Design at Centennial College. She has been an editor since 1986 and a traveller always.

ACKNOWLEDGMENTS
For photographs: Geovisuals (Kitchener, Ontario), The Canadian Tourism Commission and its photographers.
For reference: *The Canadian Encyclopedia, Encarta 1997, The Canadian Global Almanac, Symbols of Canada. Canadian Heritage*, Reproduced with the permission of the Minister of Public Works and Government Services Canada, 1997.
For maps: Promo-Grafx of Collingwood, Ont., Canada.

Library of Congress Cataloging-in-Publication Data

Beckett, Harry. 1936 -
   Prince Edward Island / by Harry Beckett.
     p. cm. — (Journey across Canada)
   Includes index.
   Summary: An introduction to the geography, history, economy, major cities, and interesting sites of Canada's smallest province.
   ISBN 1-55916-200-7 (alk. paper)
   1. Prince Edward Island—Juvenile literature. [1. Prince Edward Island.]
I. Title II. Series: Beckett, Harry, 1936 -   Journey across Canada.
F1047.4.B43 1997
971.7—dc21   97–1421
                                              CIP
                                            AC

Printed in the USA

TABLE OF CONTENTS

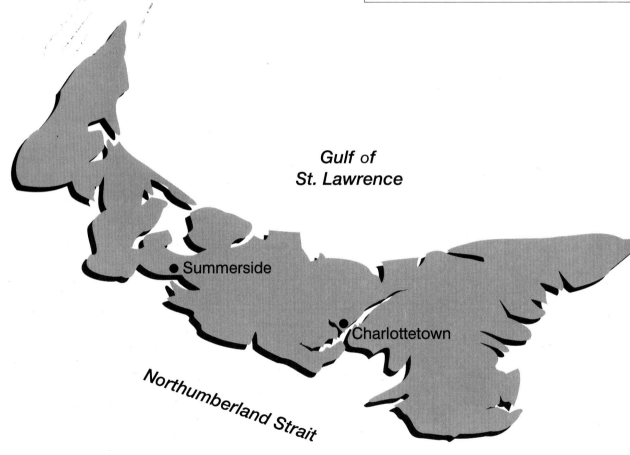

Gulf of St. Lawrence

● Summerside

● Charlottetown

Northumberland Strait

PROVINCE OF PRINCE EDWARD ISLAND

Chapter One

SIZE AND LOCATION

Prince Edward Island, usually called P.E.I., was named for the son of King George III of Britain. It is the smallest Canadian province, but has more people per square kilometre (per square mile) than any other. It is about twice the size of Rhode Island in the United States and about half the size of Jamaica.

The province is an island in the Gulf of St. Lawrence. A shallow channel, called the Northumberland Strait, separates it from the provinces of New Brunswick and Nova Scotia. The Island is reached from the mainland by ferry or a 12.9 kilometre (8 mile) long bridge, which was built in 1997.

With Nova Scotia and New Brunswick, it makes up what are called the **Maritimes** (MARE ih timez).

Find out more...

- The province is 224 kilometres (139 miles) long and 4 to 60 kilometres (2.5 to 37 miles) wide.
- The Strait is about 15 kilometres (9.3 miles) wide.

Chapter Two

GEOGRAPHY: LAND AND WATER

During the Ice Age, glaciers left behind the rich land that became P.E.I. When the ice melted and the land rose above sea level, the deep layer of reddish brown sand and clay soil for which the Island is well-known came to light.

The Island is mostly less than 60 metres (197 feet) above sea level—flat in the west, hilly in the central area, and gently rolling in the east.

P.E.I. consists of green fields and forests, with a red, sandy soil.

North shore near Cavendish

Many **estuaries** (ES choo er eez) cut into the coast. In the south and east, these form good harbours, including Charlottetown, the provincial capital. Sand banks and dunes around the north coast block the harbour mouths and allow only small boats to enter.

Chapter Three

WHAT IS THE WEATHER LIKE?

Nowhere on the Island is far from the sea. The water in the Northumberland Strait and the Gulf of St. Lawrence is quite warm. This warmth keeps the climate of the Island milder than is usual this far north.

The winters are long but not too cold. Annually, Charlottetown has 1201 millimetres (47 inches) of **precipitation** (prih sip ih TAY shun). Unlike its neighbouring provinces, P.E.I. does not get much fog.

The Strait freezes in winter, and ice-breakers have to keep the shipping lanes open. Drifting ice can cause problems for fishing boats on the Strait until May. Winds cool as they blow over the ice and to the land. This slows down the arrival of spring.

Find out more...

- The average daily temperatures are 19°C (66° F) in July and -7°C (19° F) in January.
- The summers are humid but the sea breezes cool people down.

The beach on a pleasant summer's day

8

Chapter Four

MAKING A LIVING: HARVESTING THE LAND

So much of Prince Edward Island is farmland that people call it the Million-Acre Farm. The main crop, potatoes, gives it another nickname—Spud Island. Three quarters of the crop is **exported** (ek SPORT ed) as seed potatoes. The rest is sold as table potatoes or french fries to eastern North America. Other vegetables, fruit, and tobacco are some more of the Island's crops.

Eighty percent of the Island's milk production is **processed** (PROS est) and exported.

Fishing is important to the Island. Catches are small but high in quality. P.E.I. lobsters and oysters are famous.

Not long ago, farms used workhorses. Now many have closed because of the cost of getting new machinery. Government and university research help to improve farming and fishing.

A field of potatoes

Find out more...

- P.E.I. is also called the Garden of the Gulf.
- P.E.I. sells seed potatoes to more than fifteen countries. Seed potatoes are used to grow other potatoes.

Chapter Five

FROM THE EARLIEST PEOPLES

The **Micmac** (MIK mak) peoples lived on Prince Edward Island for centuries before Jacques Cartier claimed it for France in 1534.

European ships used the island as a fishing base until French immigrants began to arrive in 1719. Thirty-nine years later, Britain took control of what is now eastern Canada and the French, the **Acadians** (uh KAY dee unz), were forced to leave.

Early fishing boats were made of wood.

A "patchwork quilt" of farmland similar to Europe

Eventually British and American settlers came.

The modern population has stayed steady. Newcomers arrive, and Islanders leave to work elsewhere. The Islanders are mostly British in background, with some Acadians and Micmac peoples.

Chapter Six

MAKING A LIVING: FROM INDUSTRY

The Island's main resources are the soil and the sea. They supply potatoes, other vegetables, and fish to the important food processing industry.

P.E.I. has minerals and natural gas deposits, but they are not big enough to develop. Making things here is expensive because many raw materials and the oil or coal to generate electricity must be brought to the Island. The bridge to the mainland will make transportation faster and cheaper.

The sea and the beautiful beaches bring many tourists to P.E.I. Tourism has also brought problems—badly controlled development and sales of land to people who don't live there.

Find out more...

- P.E.I. does produce some nuclear power.
- P.E.I.'s forests have been cleared to create farmland and for wood to build houses and ships.

Green Gables—Tourism is a major industry.

Chapter Seven
IF YOU GO THERE...

You will enjoy walking on the long, white beaches and swimming in the warm waters of the Gulf of St. Lawrence. There is also trout fishing, deep-sea fishing, and golf for nature-lovers.

In Prince Edward Island National Park, the green-roofed house of L.M. Montgomery's book Anne of Green Gables attracts thousands of visitors yearly. Historic sites in Charlottetown especially recall the role that the Island played in the Canadian **confederation** (kun fed uh RAY shun).

The Islanders celebrate their way of life with festivals. There are potato blossom festivals, strawberry festivals, oyster festivals, and lobster suppers galore.

At the strawberry festival

Find out more...

- L.M. Montgomery wrote her books about Anne in the town of Cavendish.
- Charlottetown has a summer music festival.
- The Acadian National Festival celebrates the Island's French Heritage.

Chapter Eight

MAJOR CITIES

Charlottetown, on the Northumberland Strait, is the capital of Prince Edward Island. It was founded in 1768, and named for Charlotte, the wife of King George III. The Charlottetown Conference (1864) led to the formation of Canada in 1867.

A good harbour and nearness to the mainland make this the Island's chief port. The farms of the region do their business there. Tourists like the climate, the white beaches, the harbour, and the old town.

Province House, where the idea of Canada was born

Charlottetown, the provincial capital

Summerside was a Micmac and Acadian settlement until American immigrants arrived during the American Revolution (1775-83). Shipbuilding was an early industry. Another was fox-fur farming. The construction in 1941 of Canadian Forces Base Summerside gave the town new life. Summerside serves the local farming area and is P.E.I.'s main potato-shipping port.

Chapter Nine
SIGNS AND SYMBOLS

On top of the coat of arms is the English lion from the shield of Prince Edward, the prince the Island was named after. Below it is a green island with a tree and three saplings. The large tree represents England, and the small oaks represent the province's three counties.

The flag also shows the lion, the green island, and its four trees. Red and white bands create a border on three sides.

The Latin motto, meaning "The small under the protection of the great," recalls the Island's history as a British territory.

The provincial flower, a type of orchid, is the lady's-slipper.

Prince Edward Island's flag, coat of arms, and flower

GLOSSARY

Acadians (uh KAY dee unz) — the people of the former French colony in eastern Canada; their descendants

Confederation (kun fed uh RAY shun) — provinces, states, or countries joining together

estuary (ES choo er ee) — the broad mouth of a river flowing into the sea

export (ek SPORT) — to sell or ship goods to other countries

Maritimes (MARE ih timez) — New Brunswick, Prince Edward Island, and Nova Scotia; named so because they are on the sea

Micmac (MIK mak) — a Native people of eastern Canada

precipitation (prih sip ih TAY shun) — rain, dew, or snow

process (PROS es) — to prepare or treat using a special method

Mr. Lobster

INDEX